Obscenities

Obscenities

Michael Casey

Carnegie Mellon University Press
Pittsburgh 2002

Acknowledgment is made to the following publications for poems which originally appeared in them—*America:* Learning, Road Hazard; *Choice:* For Interpreter Sergeant Tuats, On What the Army Does with Heads, Sentiment, Serious Incident Report, Slickness, Syphilis and Fort Lewis; *The Little Magazine:* Darbey's Chicken; *The Nation:* Bagley, Free Love, Hoa Binh, The LZ Gator Body Collector; *Pyramid:* Bushwhacking, Sierra Tango, To Sergeant Rock.

Obscenities was first published in 1972 as Volume 67 of the Yale Series of Younger Poets by Yale University Press, New Haven. Subsequent editions were published by Warner Paperback Library, New York, and by Ashod Press, New York.

The author and publisher extend their gratitude to Stanley Kunitz for granting permission to reprint his Foreword. The author wishes to acknowledge Jack Antreassian for his efforts over the years on behalf of *Obscenities*. The publisher would like to thank Louisa Solano of the Grolier Book Shop in Cambridge, Massachusetts, for her assistance in the production of this edition.

Library of Congress Control Number: 2001091188
ISBN 0-88748-375-5

10 9 8 7 6 5 4 3 2

For William Aiken

CONTENTS

Foreword

Michael Casey's *Obscenities* is, to my knowledge, the first signifi-
cant book of poems written by an American to spring from the
war in Vietnam, though for more than seven years, since the
passage of the Gulf of Tonkin Resolution, the American
experience—and, in particular, the experience of American
youth—has been radically transformed by that ill-starred adven-
ture. Other comparable poems out of Indo-China have foundered
in declamatory indignation or bored us with their redundance.
We can no longer respond to rhetorical flourishes and sentiments
borrowed from the poets who fought—and too often died—in
the earlier wars of the century. Casey begins as a poet with an
act of rejection. He has had the original insight and the con-
trols to produce a kind of anti-poetry that befits a kind of war
empty of any kind of glory.

"This book is not about heroes. English poetry is not yet fit
to speak of them," wrote Wilfred Owen in the stillborn Preface
found among his papers. He wanted above all to depict the
senseless horrors and inhumanity of war—"All a poet can do
today is warn"—but the scale of his compassion and the eleva-
tion of his style inevitably exalted his agonists-in-khaki. Despite
his disclaimer, the imagination at work in his poems can only
be described as heroic, subsuming his subject matter:

> Nevertheless, except you share
>> With them in hell the sorrowful dark of hell,
>> Whose world is but the trembling of a flare,
>> And heaven but as the highway for a shell,
>
> You shall not hear their mirth:
>> You shall not come to think them well content
>> By any jest of mine. These men are worth
>> Your tears. You are not worth their merriment.

The outstanding poets of World War I—Owen, Sassoon, Isaac
Rosenberg—all fought in the front lines and wrote directly of
what they knew of hell, under "the monstrous anger of the

guns." Their verse is as much a by-product of trench warfare as trench mouth or shell shock. In World War II the action climbed out of the muck into the wild blue sky or rolled across open plains and deserts in armored tanks. Mobility, automation, depersonalization marked the new order of hell, a stupefying extension of modern city life, not calculated to shock the imagination into other states of awareness. Performed at a distance, even killing lost its moral and aesthetic force. "How easy it is to make a ghost," wrote Keith Douglas. Except for the Air Force, few soldiers preserved the legend of belonging to a doomed elite. Death distributed his favors with an equal hand, converting civilians as indifferently as it did combatants into "men of dust." Often the civilian ordeal was the more harrowing. "In the fourth year of this war," observed Douglas in a posthumously published essay, "we have not a single poet who seems likely to be an impressive commentator on it." In fact, no poet—American or British—was to achieve superlative distinction or special identity from a distillation of his World War II experiences. Douglas's own admired poem on the desert war, written in Egypt shortly before Montgomery's attack, appears rather stilted and formalistic now:

> To-night's a moonlit cup
> and holds the liquid time
> that will run out in flame
> in poison we shall sup.
>
> The moon's at home in a passion
> of foreboding. Her lord,
> the martial sun, abroad
> this month will see time fashion
>
> the action we begin
> and Time will cage again
> the devils we let run
> whether we lose or win.

Randall Jarrell's war poems of the period were more vital and clever—he had the curious gift of making the whole grim business sound like a sinister fairy tale—but the irony, I fear, begins to wear a bit thin in places:

And the world ends here, in the sand of a grave,
All my wars over? . . . It was easy as that!
Has my wife a pension of so many mice?
Did the medals go home to my cat?

Unlike his predecessors, Michael Casey did not see action as either infantryman or airman. His appropriately inglorious assignment in Vietnam, given the nature of the war, was to serve in the Military Police as a highway patrolman over a thirty-mile stretch of Vietnamese National Highway One, a two-lane macadam road, and as a gate guard at LZ Bayonet, across the highway from the big Chu Lai air base. These locations provide the setting for most of the poems in this book. Specifically, LZ Bayonet was the headquarters of the 198th Infantry Brigade (commanded by a celebrated colonel, who wore the Congressional Medal of Honor and who was nicknamed The Reaper by his men) and the 6th ARVN Infantry Regiment. Some readers may want to fill in the landscape with a picture of the steep hills, pockmarked with defense bunkers, that surrounded the base and protected it from rockets. "Last year [1970] on my birthday," notes Casey in an account of his military service, "was the only time the base was mortared while I was there. Sappers hit us too then. My squad under the Sgt. Booboo of the book was sent to the headquarters building to guard it. From there I could see two of the perimeter bunkers that had been blown up by satchel charges. That day was the most war I got to see. I was lucky. Two of my friends died near my hooch then. One friend an American and the other a Vietnamese interpreter sergeant who worked for the 198th Brigade's civil affairs section."

Casey's assignment brought him into close contact with Vietnamese nationals. He made friends among them and studied their language. For this, he recalls, "I was considered a dink lover." He has strong feelings about the war, but he did not write his poems in order to exploit them as propaganda. His poems express no opinions, and the closest he comes to a generalization—

one of the few times his voice is even slightly raised—is in the lines:

> If you have a farm in Vietnam
> And a house in hell
> Sell the farm
> And go home

Obscenities is conceived as a book, not as a random collection of poems. The anectodal mode of narration that Casey has adopted is a risky one, since it calls for great energies and skill to prevent it from going slack and nerveless. In this case it works, perhaps partly because of the inherent excitement of his material, but mostly because he is a natural and frugal storyteller, not given to self-indulgence; and because he does not have to strain for credibility—his honesty shines through; and because he listens. How beautifully he listens, and with what a fine ear for speech patterns!

> Gentlemen
> One year over there
> An you'll age ten
> Am I exaggeratin, Sergeant Rock?
> You ask Sergeant Rock
> If I'm exaggeratin
>
> Sergeant Rock was in the army
> Since the day he was born
> He was in the war of the babies

I recommend reading this book straight through, from first to last, as though it were a novel or a play, in order to follow the implicit development of the action, a progress of awareness, and to make the acquaintance of a sterling cast of recurring characters, including bluff, profane Bagley; Boston Booboo, the ineffable sergeant; his Canadian counterpart, Sergeant JohnJohn, who played a dirty trick on his music-loving captain (see "Sentiment"); bereaved and spunky Stanley, one of a pair Vietnamese girls employed as police matrons, whom the men, for apparently obvious reasons, called Stanley and Ollie, after Laurel and

Hardy; and the GI named Casey, "Sort of big / Sort of doofus looking," who threads his way from episode to episode, not always announcing his presence, not always self-respectful. *Obscenities* is full of what the title suggests. War has its scatology, even its hilarity at times. This young poet enjoys his joke as much as any man. But the manifestation of the ultimate obscenity, as revealed to "The LZ Gator Body Collector," is beyond either tears or laughter:

> See
> Her back is arched
> Like something's under it
> That's why I thought
> It was booby trapped
> But it's not
> It just must have been
> Over this rock here
> And somebody moved it
> After corpus mórta stiffened it
> I didn't know it was
> A woman at first
> I couldn't tell
> But then I grabbed
> Down there
> It's a woman or was
> It's all right
> I didn't mind
> I had gloves on then

Here as elsewhere the language is so simple and open, so plausible, that one scarcely notices the artfulness of the compression, the understatement, the nice distortion of "rigor mortis," the rightness of the unpunctuated linear structure based (but not slavishly) on the short span of the breath units.

One of the last poems in this sequence is entitled "Learning." The speaker is unnamed, but we can guess his identity.

> I like learning useless things
> Like Latin

I really enjoyed Latin
Caesar and the Gallic Wars
Enjoyed his fighting
The Helvetians and Germans
And Gauls
I enjoyed Vietnamese too
The language
Its five intonations
Its no conjugations
A good language to learn
Vietnam is divided in
Three parts too
It makes me wonder
Who will write their book

I submit that Michael Casey, with his first volume of poems, has already written at least one chapter of that book.

Stanley Kunitz

Obscenities

The Company Physical Combat
Proficiency Test Average

The company average'd be higher
But Ramos there
He went inta the mile run
With a near four hundred
Burnt smoke for the first three laps
An then he got sick
Ana committee group sergeant there
Another Puerto Rican fella
Told him ta quit   ta leave
An so he got a zeero on the whole test
An that brought the company average
Down   a point ana half
    In my opinion
Ramos got fucked
He could've lowcrawled his ass
The rest a the way
An still a got a four fifty
If I'd a seed that sergeant
I'm not ascairt a nobody
I'd a beat the shit out a him
    But don't feel bad, Ramos
What's done is did
That's all right, son
Ya git another chance tomorrer
Though that don't help
The company average none

Transcribed Proof of Denial
For Arthur Dore

Mah man Blake
Yo days is numbered
They's gonna open up
An envelope
At yo house
Someday raht soon
An they jus gonna be
A lil piece of yo sorry hide
In ther   an yo girl
Gonna say   whas this hier
An Ahm gonna be ther too
To console er
In er hour o need
With mah rod of salvation
Yo dam raht
But raht now
Ahm gonna sleep
Ahm too tired
An Ahm gonna beg yo pardon
An the devil's
Fo given yo some mo tahm
To repent yo sins
But be sho now
Ta pray to the good Lord
Fo mercy   cuz Blake
Yo certain not receive none
From mah hands
So be sho now an pray
Lak as Ah says
Yo days is numbered
Morro's yo last day on earth
Fo sho
Cuz Mah man Casey's
Gonna remahn me
So as Ah won' firget

Ain' that raht, Casey
Casey?
Sheeit
Yo been sleepin
An ain' heerd a word
Ah been sayin
Don' deny it now
Ah ain' even gonna believe ya

Knowledge

When the Command Sergeant Major
Asks ya somethin
Don't get nervous or scairt
Don't get flustrated
Say to yaself
   I'm not scairt a nothin
Stand tall an speak up proud
Ya gotta know
That ya know
What ya know
Look tall
   Whip it to me, Command Sergeant Major
   Ah know ma shit
   Whip it to me

National Guardsman

I'm going to finish
Getting my degree
And get a job
With some brokerage firm
On Wall Street
When I go for my interview
They'll ask me
    What about your military obligation?
And I'll say
    All through with it
    I'm in the National Guard
And they will fight over me
The interviewers will cream in their pants
And you sorry-assed individuals
Will be in the mud
Tough shitsky you alll
I could give a sweet fuck

Riot Control School

I thought maybe
He's a guy
That puts himself
In other people's stories
Ya know   samesame Walter Mitty
So maybe it happened
To someone else and
He only stole the story
        Men
        Gentlemen
        I been in three world wars
        World War Two
        Korea
        And
        Santo Domingo
We looked at each other then
Santo Domingo???
        And let me tell you
        Gentlemen
        That was a war
        With a capital doubleyou
        They threw everything at us
            I was point man in a wedge
        Formation
        And I got hit on the head
        With a coke bottle molotov cocktail
        But
        I
        Kept
        On
        Going
        And everyone thought that
        This was all bullshit
        But I thought maybe
        It might have been

To Sergeant Rock

Gentlemen
One year over there
An you'll age ten
Am I exaggeratin, Sergeant Rock?
You ask Sergeant Rock
If I'm exaggeratin
Sergeant Rock was in the army
Since the day he was born
He was in the war of the babies

Big John

It morally destroyed me   I tell ya
Ther I was   sittin on the beach
Lyin down on my stomach
Soakin up some rays   ya know
And this weight sat on my back
And I felt some water on my back
I first thought
Someone had thrown some water on me
But no   gawdamit   but no
The bitch had actually pissed on my back
I was shocked   I tell ya
I dashed inta the water right away
Ta rinse off   and after a while
She came into the water too
An apologized to me
   Gee   I'm sorry
   I just had to do that
   Something forced me
Ya   I said   it's all right
Sure   don't worry about it
I just rather ya wouldn't do that again   I says
An   ya know   whenever I came across her
At school after that
She'd look all embarrassed
What a crazy kid   but I'm tellin ya
I never been so shocked
It absolutely destroyed my mind
Besides leavin a yellow stain on my back

Paco

When I was radio operator
I sent Paco
On a larceny
Of personal property
At headquarters
Special troops
Paco calls back on the radio
Ten-twenty that last ten-twenty-four
(Disregard, ignore, shitcan that last assignment)
The dude
Found his dust

the dude found his dust: *the soldier found his money*

Serious Incident Report:
Maltreatment of Trainee

This here sergeant's
Shit is flaky
I ain't even bullshittin
Seven willies from another unit
Seen him kick
This trainee
In the balls
An' this trainee
Is hurtin
I ain't even bulljivin
All the doctor can do
Is put ice down there
Doctor says
The dude'll
Be sterile
In at least
The left nut
Doctor says
His balls is
As flat as a pancake

willies: *trainees*

The Boogaloo

Broken arms and his chest kicked in
I felt sorry for the fucker
I ain't bullshittin
His arm sure looked funky-assed, didn't it
He used to be in the MP's, ya know
Got kicked out for goin AWOL
He's had his problems
I ain't bullshittin
Got kicked out of the MP's
An got put into that unit
Headquarters-one-five
Wouldn't say nothin about it either
Had to write it up as report of incident
Got it by a truck   he says
Cryin an screamin
His nose all over his face
Blood all over the barracks
An nobody there say nothin
    We gotta put the boogaloo
On headquarters-one-five
Ya know that, don'tcha

put the boogaloo on: *hassle, give trouble to*

Bushwhacking

There are laws against it
Against parking   and
Against indecent exposure
That doesn't make me bother them though
But rather it's
What they can do
That I can't do
They may not do
     I don't care where they park
I just want to catch them screwing
It's the fun I have
In a twelve hour day

Sierra Tango

Wild Irish Rose Wine
Quart bottle   half full
Was found unsecured
In subject's vehicle
Subject became belligerent
And directed profanity
Towards Mike Papa Armen
Such reprehensible conduct
Merited subject ride
To Provost Marshal's Office
Where subject was cited
And released to unit
On department of defense
Form six-two-niner
Subject's vehicle was secured
At scene by Mike Papas
   Did they ever whip
   His sorry ass
   Lots of stick time there

sierra tango: s and t in the phonetic radio alphabet
mike papa: m and p in the phonetic radio alphabet

Guardmount Speech

You guards in fifty
Listen up
There's a man there   Ankabrant
Someone puts the kabosh to
Ever night
Anklebrink's at the sally port
Right now   behind ya
They set his bunk on fire tonight
Yesterday they kaboshed him on the head
An threw water on him
An the day fore that
They hid his clothes under the barracks
So you guys
Watch Ankenbrink's bunk
It's the first un on the left downstairs
The duty officer
Suggest
When you fall asleep
You all fall asleep in a circle
Around Ankenbrank's bunk
That was the duty officer bein funny

guardmount: *inspection and briefing of stockade guards*
sally port: *entrance and exit gate of a stockade*

The Box Riot
Ft. Leonard Wood Stockade
July 26, 1969

They called me out of bed
For slack an I
Rushed right over there
An all sorts of rank was there
An they went with me
To the box all right
An the prisoners were all out
An I get beat up
By two box dudes
With two by fours
They was watchin real good though
We only saw one side
Only Africa and me went in there
The guards inside
Locked themselves up
So they wouldn't get hurt
And Wilkerson got hit
With a hammer
Helpin the engineers at the gate
One of the engineers
They think is dead
Ya could see inside his head
Only Africa an Wilkerson
An me was there
They started biffin us with
Two by fours
I grabbed a two by four
An started biffin them back
Christ Almighty
They not cutting me no slack
I'm not cutting them any

box: *stockade barracks for maximum security prisoners*
slack: *aid, assistance*
cut slack: *give a break*

Happiness

I'm happy
You know that?
I'm out a the box
And they're making me white hat
I feel young
I feel like I'm nineteen
No fooling
I'm glad I was drafted
When I was twenty-four
And when I'm through
I'll be twenty-six
All because
I'm out a the box
I'm really glad
I'm as happy as shit

white hat: *military police patrolman*

Birthstone

Nice ring
I'm gonna keep it for tomorrow   he says
Tomorrow's my birthday
And the ring has the same stone an everthing
   That's why I'm so proud with myself today
   I got my class ring back from Fennolds
   From Fennolds in the box
Give me my ring   I says
   I don't have your ring
You give me that ring
Right now
Today
Or I'm going to the sally port
An tellin Sergeant Tesarenski
   So he gives it to me
   After I tell that   to him
Here it is   he says
Don't you cross my path again
   An I says
I'll cross your path
Whenever I feel like it
   I said that
   And walked away
   Fast

Automatic Fire for Record

On a cold morning
Upton was my scorer
A Canadian enlisted
In our army
What a fool
   Aim for the middle targets
   Leaders stay in the middle to better
   Direct their people
   In every army in the world
   Aim for them
      And then fire to the left
   Because it's the nature
   Of the M-sixteen
   To fire to the left
   And we don't fire
   Against the nature of things
By the fiftieth round
My glasses fog up
I am only nearsighted a little
With some focusing problems
I can take them off and do
Adjusting my point of aim
A little to the right
Because what my plain eyes see
Is always a little to the right
Of where it actually should be
   Near the end
Of my two hundred rounds
I stop holding the magazine
With my left hand
And place it
Around the plastic covering
On cold mornings happiness
Is a warm gun
In cold hands

Don't be left out in the warm
Come   come come alive
Where it's freezing
The icy taste of

Welcome

Welcome to building 950
Gateway to the Pacific
Group leaders report to shipping office
No females allowed

Gentlemen
Attendance at these mandatory formations
Is of primary concern with us group leaders
I want to see all you smiling faces
With me in the big country
Also we'll be flying   on an airplane
With two young ladies   gentlemen
With two stewardesses
Ya American soldiers
An grown-up men
Construct yaselves accordingly

On What the Army Does
With Heads

Most Americans like kids
GI's is no exception
They likes to play with kids
Walking up to them
Pattin them on the head
Hey ya cute lil fucker
Now
If you see a little bald-headed kid
Don't do that
Don't go pattin him on the head
This kid's Buddhist
An it's against his religion
You do that
An to them
To these people here
You've fucked with the kid's head
An no one can
Convince that kid's mama
You didn do it on purpose

A Bummer

We were going single file
Through his rice paddies
And the farmer
Started hitting the lead track
With a rake
He wouldn't stop
The TC went to talk to him
And the farmer
Tried to hit him too
So the tracks went sideways
Side by side
Through the guy's fields
Instead of single file
Hard On, Proud Mary
Bummer, Wallace, Rosemary's Baby
The Rutgers Road Runner
And
Go Get Em—Done Got Em
Went side by side
Through the fields
    If you have a farm in Vietnam
And a house in hell
Sell the farm
And go home

track: *tracked vehicle*
TC: *track commander*

Propaganda

Female nurse Le Thi Nguyet belonging to the C95A
   company
Because discouraged of various idle promises of the
   Cong San
Has therefore rallied on the 23rd of June of the year 1970.
The Cong San propagandize that whoever rallies   will be
Killed   but to the contrary Miss Nguyet was kindly treated
And cared for by the government. Friends of the C95A,
Follow Miss Nguyet quickly. Do not follow the orders of
Leader Nguyen-Thien, for that path invites death.

Cong San: *Communists*

Prisoner of War

5-11-198
Status: Civil Defendant
Le Thi Nguyet
VC nurse
Age: 17
ID#: Negative
Place of Capture: Tuyet Diem #4
Unit of Capture: B Co 5/46
Residence: Tuyet Diem #4

Subject stated she had been
Trained as a nurse at Tuyet
Diem #4. Training lasted 10
Days. Subject stated that she
Was chosen as there was a li-
Mited number of girls in her
Village. The training was gi-
Ven by a South Vietnamese wo-
Man, aged 24, whose name sub-
Ject did not know. Subject
Stated that at Tuyet Diem #4
Were four male medics whose
Names and ages she did not
Know but who never carried weapons.
Subject could not describe
The type of weapons which the
Male medics did not carry.
Subject was taught to change
Bandages and treat minor cuts
But was given no medical sup-
Plies upon completion of
Training. Subject did not know
Of VC/NVA activities in vicinity

Of her village. Subject will
Be sent to Binh Son for fur-
Ther interrogation by Vietna-
Mese National Police.

The POW Cage and the Hoi Chanh Rallier

The Chieu Hoi
Walks through the gate
With Dutch behind him
Dutch's M-sixteen on his hip
And at the door of the shack
Bagley gives a great big smile
And yells welcome
Throwing his arms out wide
Then Bagley goes and shakes
The kid's hand
And the Chieu Hoi
Gets the happiest look on his face
This kid has just seen Santa
Bagley portraying Santa here
The kid doesn't really understand Bagley
The kid doesn't understand English
But for us
Bagley keeps on with his act
   Now
     I'll tell ya what I'm gonna do
     Kid
     If ya play ya cards right
     Ya can be a Kit Carson scout
     And be a point man
     For the United States Grunts
     And
     While that might be fun
     I kindly fuckin doubt it
     But
     It's just another one
     Of the many bennies

In today's action army
Hey
Kid
This fuckin army's allll right

Hoi Chanh: *Communist deserter*
Chieu Hoi: *open arms program to encourage Communist desertions*
Kit Carson scout: *guerilla who has changed sides*
Grunts: *infantrymen*
bennies: *benefits*

Darbey's Chicken

Ever since one of the mess hall girls
Gave Darb that chicken
I been goin out of my mind
Its peepin was drivin me crazy
I swear
Two seconds couldn't go by
Without the thing peepin
Fifty times
And Darb would've
Married the thing
I swear
If it wasn't a different
Race of animal
He was real happy about having it
Like once
When it snuck under the cage shack
Where the rats live
You could hear the thing
Not peeping
But screaming and squawking
Like it was getting killed
An I'm thinkin
This is cool
This is no more chicken week
But no
The thing walks into the hooch then
Peeping
An pecking at the floor
Ruffling its feathers
And Darb says real proud-like
Scratch one rat
But now
That's all over
Darbey's going mad
He's looking all over for his chicken
But he can't find it nowhere

And I know where his chicken is
I introduced his chicken
To H Troop's pig, Dorothy
Dorothy ate it
Pigs are tougher than rats
Tougher than chickens too

For the Old Man

The old man was mumbling
And Delbert was shouting at him
Im! Im! Im!
Until Booboo told Delbert
To shut the fuck up
The old man was skinny
The old man had looked young
With the sand bag
Over his head
Without the bag
The man was old
There was a bump
The size of a grapefruit
On his head
When the bag was taken off
The man
Clasped his hands
In front of him
And bowed to us
Each in turn
To Booboo, Delbert, and me
He kept it up too
He wouldn't stop
His whole body shaking
Shivering with fright
And somehow
With his hands
Clasped before him
It seemed as if
He was praying to us
It made all of us
Americans
Feel strange

im: *silence*

Phuong Hoang

I never cared to learn the language
I don't want to make friends here
I don't want to think about them later

I'm getting relieved of duty here
You know?
Being sent to division
It doesn't bother me
Why should it
I'm to be here one year anyway
You heard of the phoenix program   heh?
I will not touch the stuff
They sent me to two phoenix schools too
In Vung Tau
Via Air America
I went
Just for my own edification   heh?
For my own reasons   you know?
Elimination
CIA idea
All CIA   heh?
The whole thing here
A CIA   thing gone wild
Heaven help them in hell   heh

phuong hoang: *phoenix; program for hiring agents to kill Communist civilian leaders*

33

For Interpreter Sergeant Tuats

Awwwwwww
Too bad, Tuats
Toots
Tootsy
Poor Tootsy
Won't be able
To visit
The An Tan skivvy girls
Tonight
Too bad, Tuats
Ya gonna
Hafta translate
These documents
All night long
Tough shit, Tootsy
Sure wish
I could help ya
I'll give the girls ya regards
Ahhhh   yes
A big cat'll scratch ya ta death
But a little pussy
Never hurt anyone

Boston Booboo or
The POW Cage Visit

In the security squad shack
Booboo was at the desk
Showing
A homely Vietnamese farm girl
A skin magazine
He sees a Japanese girl
In the mag
Points to the picture
And points to the girl
Number one
Samesame
Says Booboo
And the girl giggles
And says
Number one
Over and over
Booboo says to me
She thinks
American girls are too fat
Ya know these farm girls
She's a strong girl
She is
You should see her fill sandbags

number one: *good, best, most preferred*

Slickness

You
Think
You're slick
I says to him
You
Think
You're tough
Go ahead
Go head
Hit me
Hit me
Hit me
And the ass-hole
He hit me

Message in the Public Interest

Happiness
Is when
The person
You hate most
In the whole world
Gets the clap
So if you think
You
Have VD
The burning
The dripping
Sensation
See the medic
At your aid station
Right now
And
Stay out
Of the Yucatan Rain Forest
This is the
Armed Forces Vietnam Network
The best of music
Here
From everywhere
From Monkey Mountain

The Death Truck

Yellow flags with three red stripes
Flowers
Wreaths
Banners
And
Smell
Mark
The death truck
I
Never
Seen
One
Stop

27th Surgical Hospital

The honcho nurse there
Hates dinks
This head nurse
Always hassles me
When I bring one in
The first thing
She asks me is
 Is he a combat casualty?
 Hell no, lady
 This dink just
 Got hit by a truck
 An American truck
 That beat feet after hitting him
 An he bleeding
 All over my spit shine
 Take him to the Vietnamese hospital in An Tan
The woman don't realize
That it's far away
That her hospital's closer
That blood makes me sick

honcho: *leader*

Ackerfield

The National Police Captain
Slapped the soul brother
And drew his forty-five
Locking and loading it
A PF nearby
Pulled a pin from a grenade
And held it high
Ack and JohnJohn
Stood between the pistol and the GI
Ack had his M-sixteen
On autogetem
And JohnJohn had
Only his M-seventy-nine
And JohnJohn
Says to Ack
"Ack,
   I don't got
   Any cannister
   For this,
   Just AG"
"Thump one"
   "I'm hep" says John

PF: *Popular Forces, Vietnamese Government Militia*
autogetem: *automatic*
M-seventy-nine: *grenade launcher*
cannister: *pellet round*
AG: *grenade round*

Off Limits

Must've been three miles
Down that road by Arty Hill
What with Arty Hill
Sending up red flares an all
Must've been fifty PFs
Round him
With carbines mostly
Some M-fourteens too
Girl PFs too
With carbines and tennis shoes
White tennis shoes
A PF   with an orange sports shirt
An golf cap was with a radio
He must've told the An Tan PFs
An all these PFs
Around the one scared soul brother
Just tryin to get a piece a pussy mann
Why's everyone so cold   mannn
Must be some policy   mannnn
Against a rapport with the people
There it is home   I says
Mah name's
Spec four John Fogarty
Military Pohlice
Ah can an will be
One nahce guy an
One mean sonovabitch
Yawl under apprehension
Fa bein off limits
Yawl ware of yo rahts
Under Article Thirty-one
A the Uniform Code
A military justice?

red flares: *indication of enemy within a base's perimeter*
Article Thirty-one: *U.S. Army's Fifth Amendment*

To Miss Thanh

She used to work
At the officer's club
And she was very pretty
So she made a lot of money there
I told her
    You ain't even giving me anything, young lady
But my girl friend
Gave me a little gold ring anyway
That I wear sometimes even now
Just as fine
A girl
As she could want to be
And after raiding
The whore houses
Every night
It was nice
To go visit
My fifteen year old
Girl friend
And
Hold
Hands

First Sight

Seeing it
Nothing could
Convince me
That it would not move again
And I stared at it
Until Gregory slapped me
Then we got Castro
Who had been chasing
A bird with a yellow head
And Hieu
("beaucoups VC Quang Ngai
  VC of very poor quality")
And in our jeep
We beat feet
We
Not having a radio that month
Left it to the flies
A little while longer

Quang Ngai: *Vietnamese province with capital city of the same name*

Mourning

Stanley's father
Was a hamlet chief
For the government and
So   being an enemy of the people
He was blown up by a grenade
(I told Bagley that
   Papasan should have gone
   To the Cong San village chief school
   As well as the Cong Hoa school)
So after this
Stanley came to work
As police matron
With a white towel
About her hair
For Bagley this was a time
To mess with Stanley
And he started messing
With her hair
Stanley turned around
And kneed him between his legs
If someone messes with the head
Of a person in mourning
She might not be able
To talk with her papasan again
When the man
Who can talk
To the dead
Comes to her village
As it turned out though
Bagley did not mess with Stanley's head
Enough
She was able to talk to her father
Her father
She told me

Had told her
He was in a place
Of very poor quality
The Vietnamese equivalent of hell

Cong San: *Communist*
Cong Hoa: *Republic*

Autogetem

If it looks like
The thing's gonna be equal
It's no fight week
For these dudes
But now
If they catches Charlie
A little bit
Light on his ass
They ain't even cuttin no slack
An they's a bunch
Of gung ho mothers
Each an every one of em
'll have his M-sixteen
On autogetem

Explanation

My friend with me is National Policeman Hieu
Of the National Police Field Force
Hieu shakes his head and says something
In Vietnamese meaning   of very poor quality
My friend is impressed
Not favorably, I think,
As the Marine Captain
Explains the key chain
On which is a bit of jawbone
With three little teeth
He points to it
"VC" he says

"I could've guessed"
I says, "that a Communist
Would have but three teeth
Three is a number
I never liked"

And the captain
Explains to me
That the thing
Was part of
A larger bone
Containing more
Than three teeth

Free Love

There the love is free
Go to Thailand;
Tokyo and Sydney
'd be bad for you there,
Man   there are whores
Everywhere
But a neon city whore
Costs more than more money
In Thailand you
Can get a whore
Costing money
Without it costing your soul
The girl will love you there
And it's nice
My girl cried when I left her

On Death

School children walk by
Some stare
Some keep on walking
Some adults stare too
With handkerchiefs
Over their nose
A woman
Sits on the pavement
Beside
Wails
And pounds her fists
On pavement
Flies all over
It   like made of wax
No jaw
Intestines poured
Out of the stomach
The penis in the air
   It won't matter then to me   but now
I don't want in death to be a
Public obscenity like this

Road Hazard

Eddie throws an old poncho
We found   on the ruins of LZ Gator
Over most of it
And drags it to the side of the road
I pick up the loose hand
A right hand
That is still warm
Because of the sun
And go to the side of the road
To tuck it
Under the right side
Of the poncho
With my being a Cong Giao
I think of making the sign
Of the cross but don't
Want to appear weak
To my public   the Nuoc Mau
Citizens standing around this scene
Holding their noses
We   Eddie and I
Go back to the jeep
Where Hieu was waiting all this time
With a handkerchief over his nose
I still am having
What poker face I have on
But Hieu still pats me on the shoulder
And says   okay   okay   no sweat no sweat
And I'm put out that
He doesn't do likewise to Eddie
Maybe I did appear the weakling

LZ: *landing zone, army base with a helicopter landing zone*
Cong Giao: *Catholic*

The LZ Gator Body Collector

See
Her back is arched
Like something's under it
That's why I thought
It was booby trapped
But it's not
It just must have been
Over this rock here
And somebody moved it
After corpus morta stiffened it
I didn't know it was
A woman at first
I couldn't tell
But then I grabbed
Down there
It's a woman or was
It's all right
I didn't mind
I had gloves on then

Sweetheart

Kid
Ya
Could've been
Big time
Could've been
Up there
In lights
Sweetheart
Boston
Broadway
The *National Geographic* even
But
Ya missed
Ya chance
Doll
And I have ta leave ya now
Can't wait all day
Love
And I leave ya
A pack of gum
Anyways
Cuz I like the way
You hide behind trees
Keep hiding from Americans, Sweetheart

Sentiment

Ralph
Our platoon leader
Used to play
His harmonica
All day
In between reading
Science fiction
And the *National Review*
   Ralph was the one
Who injected milk
From a hypodermic
Squirting all over
The face of our
Psych-visiting desk
Sergeant JohnJohn
JohnJohn, a Canadian,
Was on his second tour
Had driven a gun jeep
In the A Shau Valley
During his first tour
That had sort of messed him up
JohnJohn was legally
On librium at the time
Of Ralph's little joke
And so he didn't
Get too upset
But to get even
He did sneak away
The Captain's harmonica
And rubbed it up his
Ever after this
Ralph could never
Understand how much
We enjoyed his mistake-free
Home Sweet Home
But then he always knew
His men were sentimental

Back Door Man

I'm prepared but
I'm a bit overloaded
As the seventeen year old PF
Leads the way
Got my two dictionaries
One Anh-Viet
One Viet-Anh
And gas mask
And bandages
My helmet too and handcuffs
Got my stick
My gas grenade
My forty-five and
My M-sixteen
I strangle myself
On low flying clotheslines
And trip on the old French
Railroad ties
To fall into a garbage pit
I walk into a sty
Fifty dogs start to bark
And only one bites
A million chickens run away
It's a long way
To the back door
Of a skivvy girl house

Bagley

I was talking
To one of the
Chu Lai pigs
At the gate there
An he said
Some of the
Bayonet pigs
Caught him
In a skivvy girl house
Last night
An he accused
One of us
Of pointing
A weapon at him
I asked him
What did the dude look like?
And he said
   I don't know
   Sort of big
   Sort of doofus looking
An I knew right away
It was you, Casey

Learning

I like learning useless things
Like Latin
I really enjoyed Latin
Caesar and the Gallic Wars
Enjoyed his fighting
The Helvetians and Germans
And Gauls
I enjoyed Vietnamese too
The language
Its five intonations
Its no conjugations
A good language to learn
Vietnam is divided in
Three parts too
It makes me wonder
Who will write their book

The Funky People

Those air force guys are slick
They don't want
No funky army guys
At their snack bar
They got two snack bars
One all by itself
For the funky people
And it was a bummer
I couldn't wash anywhere
Athletes feet
Ringworm crotch
Dry rot armpits
Every once in a while
You know   we'd go to the ocean
In nothing but our firesticks
And there we'd get the chance
To fight the jelly fish
That are two feet deep
And it's a bummer
Trying to lather soap
In salt water   and jelly fish

AK-47

It was late
And we got stuck
Down the lurp range road
Bringing
You know whose
Girl friend back home
Krackkrackkrack
We heard and we started
Beating feet
Hauling ass
Scared shitless
I might say
I was driving
So I didn't have
That much time to think
The little people
In the back of the jeep
They fired back first
Long with his thirty-eight
And Hau with his M-sixteen
Bagley didn't do that cool
One of Hau's ejected rounds
Went down his neck
And he thought he was hit
He dropped his rifle
From the jeep
And we didn't even stop
To look for same
I hope he has to pay for it
Teach him some humility
He still thinks
He's war-wounded
From that sniper bullet
That graze-burned
His skin on the middle of his back

But didn't even leave no holes
In his shirt
I might believe that
But I kind of doubt it

AK-47: *Communist-made rifle*
Lurp: *LRRP, long range reconnaissance patrols*

Ruins

This little girlsan
From Nuoc Mau
Was playing on the ruins
Of Gator
And stepped on a mine
It blew her leg off
Below the knee
It wasn't too nice
I brought her to the medic's
From the Nuoc Mau aid station
And I brought her back home later
Hieu led the way
He drew his forty-five
Locked and loaded it too
This was the town
Closest to Bayonet
So this on Hieu's part
Surprised me
I locked and loaded
My M-sixteen though
Which was hard
My carrying the little girl
This little girlsan
From Nuoc Mau

Hoa Binh

August thirty-first
Stanley was all excited
She just made eighteen
And got to vote
For the first time
There were sixteen slates
To vote for
In Vietnam that year
And every slate's poster
Said that
That slate
Wanted Hoa Binh
From voting
She came back to me
All excited
Casee
I vote for Hoa Binh
That's nice, Stanley
I did   too
Back in Hoa Ky
I hope your vote counts

hoa binh: *peace*
Hoa Ky: *United States*

Syphilis and
Fort Lewis

OK
You dudes all think
Ya can go home now
Fuck no
The medics gotta check you out
Gotta check with your
VNPCOD
See if it was far enough back
You men
Don't know what your VNPCOD was?
It's your Vietnamese pussy cut off date